Why Am I So Crap?

Peter Williams

O&U
Onwards & Upwards

Onwards and Upwards Publishers

4 The Old Smithy, London Road, Rockbeare,
Exeter, EX5 2EA, United Kingdom.
www.onwardsandupwards.org

First edition, published in the United Kingdom by Onwards and Upwards Publishers (2019).

ISBN:	978-1-78815-505-2
Typeface:	Calibri
Graphic design:	LM Graphic Design

The views and opinions expressed in this book are the author's own, and do not necessarily represent the views and opinions of Onwards and Upwards Publishers or its staff. Every effort has been made to track down sources. Please notify the author or publisher if there are errors and omissions and these will be rectified.

Scripture quotations marked (ESV) are from the ESV® Bible (The Holy Bible, English Standard Version®), copyright © 2001 by Crossway, a publishing ministry of Good News Publishers. Used by permission. All rights reserved. Scripture quotations marked (NKJV) are taken from the New King James Version®. Copyright © 1982 by Thomas Nelson. Used by permission. All rights reserved. Scripture quotations marked (NIVUK) are taken from the Holy Bible, New International Version® Anglicized, NIV® Copyright © 1979, 1984, 2011 by Biblica, Inc.® Used by permission. All rights reserved worldwide. Scripture quotations marked (NLT) are taken from the Holy Bible, New Living Translation, copyright © 1996, 2004, 2007, 2013 by Tyndale House Foundation. Used by permission of Tyndale House Publishers, Inc., Carol Stream, Illinois 60188. All rights reserved.

Endorsements

Church Elder and Senior Partner for a doctors' practice, Peter Williams, challenges the 'if only' and comparison culture of today's society. This book is just right for you if you want to ponder the influences that shape your life. Peter looks at who we are in God's eyes; how we are loved and valued by him. Exploring what this means for those who seek to live positive and healthy lives. Asking all the right questions, it helps us to affirm that we are not indeed 'hopeless' or 'crap' but instead have the capacity to be all that God will transform us into.

Natalie Worsfold
Assistant Curate in Training
St Anne's & St Peter's
Marsh & Micklefield in the Wycombe Deanery

Dr Williams sheds light on a question which most of us secretly ask ourselves and does it with wisdom and good humour. This little book will make you feel better and give you practical advice to move forward.

Peter Saunders
CEO of IMCDA

This book is a great prescription to the lies we tell ourselves; it will help you work out God's true view of yourself

Andrew Davies
Church Planter

Why Am I So Crap?

Contents

For Pamela.

Who, when my head droops,
points me back to Jesus.

I love you.

Foreword by Rev. Rob Harris

I've known Pete for the last 30 years and it would never have crossed my mind that he would ever consider himself to be crap! Stepping out into this area with such honesty and integrity and allowing himself to be this vulnerable only goes to prove he is far from it. Pete has a heart for people and a desire to reach out to them and help make a difference that will change their lives for the better. A medical thesis, of which Pete is more than capable of writing, would have been read by few; I hope this book will be read by many, from every walk of life, who wake up daily feeling they are crap. Hopefully, by the time they have read this book and done the reflection it suggests, they will start to see themselves in a whole new light. Maybe they will even begin to seek and trust the one who said, "I have come that you may have life, and have it to the full." – Jesus Christ. He is the one I know Pete has trusted over many years in both the easy and the hard times of life.

Rev. Rob Harris
South Craven Baptist Minister

Why Am I So Crap?

Introduction

The world is constantly telling us that we aren't good enough.

- The TV shows us houses we will never be able to afford, and cars we will never have the opportunity to drive.
- Social media constantly pops up with the great days people have had, or the new shiny bicycle they have bought, or the fantastic cake they have made, or, worst of all, their amazing children.
- Billboards show us the beautiful clothes we could wear, if only we had the perfectly toned body to slip into them.
- Friends show us their newly decorated houses, and their stylish holiday snaps.
- Church members tell us how they got healed or beat their addiction.
- Our children tell us that all the other kids in their class have the latest iPhones and stay up till midnight watching the 42-inch LED TVs in their bedrooms.

As we are bombarded by this in all our waking hours, we gradually start to believe the lie that we are not good enough and, worse, that we will never be. At the same time, the world tells us the lie that we *could* be if...

The way this happens is subtle. We are attacked on so many fronts at the same time. In this book I want to go on an adventure together to look at these issues, and explore our natural responses to them, as well as how we can start to think differently.

This book is not to be read and put away, but to be written on and highlighted and gone back to as you come up against the feeling that you are less good than you feel you should be.

1

Why Is Everyone Better Than Me?

I was supposed to be praying, and I found myself asking, "Why am I so crap?"

I was juggling a lot of stuff in life, and it felt like I was dropping some of the balls, and that's what I asked God. His reply was not a "yes, you are". He would have had a right to say so, as he is of course perfection, but he replied, "Are you?"

In the next half an hour God clearly spoke to me and led me through some questions which I needed to address. At the end I started to gain a little perspective.

So I want to start with some questions for you.

Do you tell yourself...

- I am so rubbish?
- I am so fat?
- I will never be _____?
- I am so ugly?
- I will never achieve?
- I will never escape from this sin?
- If only I was like _____ [insert name], then...?

It always seems to be that we are not the best. We repeatedly tell ourselves this.

You might think you don't, but you do!

And we hear it all the time in so many ways.

You might think you don't, but you do!

If you never tell yourself these things, you are 100% secure in your identity, and have no need to read on. The other 99.99% of us might find some things out from what follows in this book.

It is now forty years since I started school. Goodness, that makes me feel old! I remember the stars on the tally chart on the wall, and the competition to get more than anyone else. I remember the rainbow reading books, where everyone wanted to get past the colours of the rainbow, onto the bronze, silver and gold books. If you did, you got to go through the curtain, into the junior school, to get a choice of a book from their library. We were cajoled into trying to be the first to get that particular honour.

Nothing has changed in forty years, apart from the fact that the competitiveness is now greater than it has ever been. We are now told we are all winners, so that we will feel the competition less. However, no one actually believes that, and the whole culture tells us that we must be a winner if we want to achieve anything in life.

It doesn't matter which bit of our lives we look at, we are constantly told that.

When you are at school, your parents or teachers never congratulate you if you are bottom of the class. Even the very fact there is a bottom of the class tells us something of the value we place on achieving things.

We finish school and enter the workplace, and there are juniors and seniors, and managers and bosses. There is a hierarchy of importance, it seems, and so we are in effect told every day, we are less than the best.

Perhaps you are the boss, so you have made it. Congratulations. So does that make you the most important? Where is there to progress to? Do you have anything to improve?

Perhaps now you are the boss to the bosses, and live in the biggest house on the street, with the flashiest car, with your kids going to the best school... but you still aren't in charge.

Perhaps you are now the prime minister. You have reached the top of the pile. You are boss over all the bosses. Is there anywhere to go? Do you have any room for improvement? Surely even the US President sometimes says to himself, "Oh, I got that one wrong, I must try to do that better next time."

The big question is, is it true?

Do you need to be better, bigger, faster, cleverer, more amazing than you actually are already? Does it matter where you rank – and, in fact, does the ranking even matter?

Pop stars tell us things in their songs all the time. How love should be. They don't sing about being happily married, settled down, and having two children (that would perhaps make for a very mundane song). No, they are always being left, and hurting, or leaving someone they did not love enough. They are singing about the stuff in life that makes us hurt or feel like we are in heaven. The extremes of emotions. The everyday does not sell records because it is, well, everyday!

Pop stars often sing about what it means to be successful. They would never sing about driving a Fiesta. It's always a Ferrari. Would it have been sensational if Oasis had put a Morris Marina in the swimming pool for the front cover of *Be Here*

Now? The cover was the epitome of the excesses of the 1990's. The swimming pool was previously owned by a *Playboy* executive, and at the time the band were using lots of cocaine. Despite being famous and costing a lot to produce, the album was never as successful as their former works.

Ironically a lot of this stems from pop stars' own insecurity. Despite their success we find many stars are not happy and are looking for fulfilment. Many try to escape via drinking, taking drugs, or through relationships. But they fail and regularly end up depressed and committing suicide.

Yet despite that, we want to emulate them; to look like them or have the same things they have.

The fact is, we don't.

The fact is, we are who we are.

The fact is, you are not the top, or the bottom, of whatever it is you are using as your measure of success right now.

The fact is, the fact that you are measuring it says something about the way you are thinking.

Stop for a moment.

On the opposite page, write a list of the things you do well. And the things you want to be better at.

I'm really rather good because...

_____   _____

_____   _____

_____   _____

_____   _____

_____   _____

_____   _____

_____   _____

I'd be better if...

_____   _____

_____   _____

_____   _____

_____   _____

_____   _____

_____   _____

_____   _____

Which was your longer list?

_____

What does that say about your self-esteem?

_____

What does it say about your values?

_____

_____

What does God say about the items on your list?

_____

_____

When you look at your list it probably has lots of things on both sides that make feelings rise up inside you. And that may be part of the problem. A lady in my small group at church said, "We operate on our feelings, not in God's love." Being secure in God's love helps us to be freer from the feelings that drive us to perform.

When we see others being successful it drives us to work harder. The Australian speaker and writer, Christine Caine, said, "Someone else's success does not rob you of anything." But the thing is, whilst their success does not rob us of anything, our responses can rob us of lots of things that God has on offer for us.

2

Why Do We Think What We Do?

If we get told something often enough, then we start to believe it!

Nicknames can be quite bland, but they can have a long-term impact, without you knowing it.

Captain Mark Phillips, the husband of Princess Anne, was known in the army as "Fog", because he was thick and wet! This features in news articles about him now, and even is on his Wikipedia page. He has not been in the army for over forty years, but he is stuck with the nickname Fog. Nicknames can be terribly difficult for us and can affect the way we think about ourselves.

If you were always known as dopey, then you might start to feel you are a bit slow. Then on the occasion that you are a bit slow, your subconscious tells you that of course you are slow, you are dopey.

As a teenager, my brother called me fatty. He still does sometimes, and we are now grown up with our own children. Of the three children in the family, I have carried the most weight, and my brother and sister are stick thin. At my largest I just crept into the overweight weight range, so never too big really. I am in the lowest 25% of weight of people my age, and so cannot be classed as a fatty. However, I am completely self-conscious about the inch or two you can see. Being a MAMiL (Middle Aged Man in Lycra) it is sometimes quite obvious that you can see a bit. My daughter would rib me for that, and she doesn't know what my brother has called me. So I start to worry that my weight will balloon, and watch my food and exercise more, even though no one actually believes I am fat, including me... or do I, deep down?

You see, having been told something so frequently it sticks with you. You have to be told the opposite far more often to undo what you have started to believe. People are not going to keep saying to me, "Oh Peter, you look so slim," and so it's unlikely that this will be easily undone. So the only thing that reinforces my perception of weight is the occasional comment, or seeing my MAMiL figure in the mirror, and that only tells me, they were right.

Thomas was known as the doubter after he asked to see Jesus in the flesh. He was always probably trying to live that down as he lived his life. Peter was known as the denier, after he denied Christ three times and heard the cock crow. I am sure they were often reminded of this. The thing is, they did not let this define them. If you look at what they did from that point on, they clearly were not living as their nicknames would suggest. Thomas is reputed to have travelled as far as India spreading the gospel and so is patron saint of India, and Peter had a big impact in the establishment of the church in the first century and was known for having been crucified in Rome for his faith, upside down.

We need to be careful what names we label people with. We don't know what long term changes we can make to people's psyche when we continually use the same name for them. When we say something to others, even in jest, it can have a big impact on them. If you regularly say to your friend, "You're mad," they will start to believe it, and perhaps they will start to act in that way.

The challenge, of course, is not believing what people tell us. So the big question is, what is true and how do we believe that instead?

What is/was your nickname?

_____

What does it make you believe about yourself?

_____

_____

_____

What could you do to counteract that?

_____

_____

_____

It's not just nicknames, but the people who have authority over us. So at school or work we have people around us that tell us things they think about us.

What did your teachers tell you?

_____

_____

What does your boss tell you?

_____

_____

What do your colleagues tell you?

_____

_____

What do your friends tell you?

_____

_____

Do you believe it?

_____

A teacher told me I'd never get a pass at Physics GCSE and, furthermore, that I'd never become a doctor as I was not clever enough. Now, my IQ is not that high. A bit over average. My dad, brother and sister, however, all have a genius IQ. And I know that. It's a fact. It's been measured. I am a wee bit above average, but not a high-flyer. I knew this when my teacher told me that. I could have reacted a couple of ways, and one of them was to quit.

However, I wanted to be a doctor, and I believed that God had told me that I would be. So I worked hard, and I got an A in Physics, and went on to do it at A-level. I then dropped it as a subject. I was doing four subjects, and I found Physics a bit boring and pointless, thinking about what I wanted to do, so I dropped it.

In my A-levels I could have been considered to fail. I got a B and 2 C's.

And you ask, how on earth did you get into medical school?

Well, I had been given a 3C offer. So I knew what I needed. It was a backup offer, and the place I really wanted to go to required 3 A's.

At the time my parents' business was struggling a bit, and I was working to help them. I even worked till midnight on the night before one of the exams. So I invested where it seemed important at the time.

The day came for the results, and we got up early from where we were on holiday and drove to Hereford where I had been at Sixth Form College. I went in to collect the results, and to say I was devastated was an understatement. I went out to the car where the whole family were waiting and explained to them that I had failed.

The thing was, I had not failed. I had passed with grades many would have been happy with. But I was just not top of the class.

In hindsight, I am really happy. The university I ended up at was, in my eyes, a much better university. While I was there, I had some amazing experiences with many great Christians and churches. We experienced a mini revival that saw the university described in the university's manual like this:

> For a secular university UCL certainly has a very active Christian Union.

The thing is, God knew.

Did I get adequate results?

No, I got the perfect results for what God had planned for me.

A friend of mine recently competed in the London marathon. He did not go quite as fast as he had hoped, and he messaged, "It was the heat that defeated me."

In fact, it was the hottest London marathon ever, and he was twelve minutes faster than ten years previously. That's a huge success, but he described it negatively because it was not quite what he wanted.

However, he was not the only one at it that day. Mo Farah did it in two thirds of my friend's time. He was disappointed at his slow time and that he had not broken the world record.

My friend would have been ecstatic with that time, as would every other runner in the race, but Mo believed he could do better and be the fastest man ever!

How we compare ourselves is so important. We often focus on the negative, rather than the positives that we could describe ourselves with. I am sure Mo Farah could have said that he was really proud to have won such a prestigious race, and that he hoped in the future that with more favourable weather he might even have the privilege of breaking the world record.

We make comparisons all the time. If I look at my runner friend, he is not just a runner but could beat me in all three disciplines of a triathlon, something I am trying to train for currently. That does not make me rubbish but makes him really rather sporty. He also skis better than me and can programme complex databases that I don't even pretend to understand. However, I bet I could thrash him at croquet! We need to learn to delight in other people's wonderful talents, rather than reflect that we don't quite have their positive attributes.

I was always the last one chosen in PE for the team sports. Maybe you were too. Most teams would have probably preferred that I was just on the side-line, as I could do less damage there. They would be shocked, I am sure, to see me cycling round the Peak District these days dressed in Lycra. My daughter would only comment, "As long as you don't come to collect me dressed like that!"

You see, all the time people tell us things that have influence on our thinking, and so then often on our behaviour too. We get influenced by the aside comment from someone, the implication of which they would never have meant, rather than focussing on the true facts of the situation.

What we need to do is to change our language. This will then help us to change our thinking. If you were struggling to lose weight you might have said to yourself, or even out loud, "I can't lose weight!" But it would be better if what we say is, "No wonder I never lose weight if..." We also need to remember to change our language in this way when we are talking to others.

The Bible describes two things that, in a way, are a paradox. Romans 3:23 says:

For everyone has sinned; we all fall short of God's glorious standard.

Romans 3:23 (NLT)

This could be paraphrased, "I'm not just crap, but totally crap. Every bit of me…"

Fortunately, Paul does not stop there. He goes on to say:

Now, most people would not be willing to die for an upright person, though someone might perhaps be willing to die for a person who is especially good. But God showed his great love for us by sending Christ to die for us while we were still sinners.

Romans 5:7-8 (NLT)

So God now does not look on us as bad, or worthless, but was prepared to let his Son die for us that we might be able to be united with him again. When God looks at us, he does not see us as crap, but sees us as he sees Christ, perfect.

You are perfect!

3

Do I Need to Just Apply Myself More?

Most New Year's resolutions have been broken by about the second week of the year. But we still keep making them. There are even websites to give you ideas about what you could do and how you could achieve it.

All through the year we may decide that if I _____, then I would be so much better. We constantly strive to improve ourselves in this or that way.

If only I could/would _____, then _____.

And there lies the issue. The things we strive to do are usually positive things, but we attach to them a "then"...

Then, when we don't achieve the goal we have set, or the thing does not happen, it's all our own fault because we did not try hard enough.

I believe we need to look at what success is, and then we can start to see where we need to try and where we can give ourselves a bit of a break!

So what is success?

Some people may say that I have made a success of my life. I did pretty well at school and went to university. I became a doctor. As a doctor, I have my own business and have been elected to lead the doctors in my county three times. My practice has an outstanding rating. I got married to a beautiful, popular and sensitive woman who knows and loves Jesus. We have two children, who also are doing well at school and have lots of interests and talents. I am a leader in the church to which I belong. I have the latest phone. I have done a triathlon. I have travelled all over the world and have seen so many of the amazing things that there are to see, including living in Africa with the family, working with the church there. This is success by most people's criteria.

But did I deserve all that? Plenty of people work harder and have a lot less stuff. Does that make them less of a success? No. It's makes me very privileged, and I count myself very fortunate.

But someone with no legs who masters the use of artificial limbs will have succeeded; someone who struggles to read who reads a page will have been successful. Are these things any less a success? No.

We measure success in a narrow way. We look at what is bigger, better, richer, more well-known. Perhaps this is no success at all. But we use it all the time as our measure of success. Then, when we don't reach that level, we are upset that we are a failure.

We often tell ourselves, "I'd be so much better if _____."

My school reports often had the phrase, "Peter could do so much better if". I am sure with enough work I could get a degree in astrophysics, but why would I want to? There are probably some people whom God has called into an area where they need such a degree. I am grateful that clever people know how to put satellites into orbit and that makes my life easier and more productive. But that's not what God has called me to do. So I don't need to work hard on astrophysics. (There are many things in life we can be thankful for!)

I am thankful for good health, but I spend a lot of time explaining to people how it would be beneficial to them to strive a little to have a better diet or lose some weight in order to have better health. I often say the "if" word when I am doing that. I would argue that taking care of the temple that God has given us, our body, is quite important and demands a bit of effort on our part sometimes.

Like school reports, we often in working life get feedback on our performance. Quite often these assessments will have lots of positives but may contain some negatives. Where do we put our focus straight away? On the negative thing. Now that may be important, and we may benefit from reviewing our behaviour and attitudes. It may be that we could be better in a particular area. God has an uncanny knack of honing and changing us little by little.

When we hear or spot the negative, that's when we resolve to work harder, do more, and then we tell ourselves that then success will come...

So do we need to work harder? Or do we assume that it's all down to chance and so not bother with anything. Ecclesiastes says:

> *Of making many books there is no end, and much study wearies the body.*
>
> *Ecclesiastes 12:12 (NIVUK)*

That does not mean we should not study. If I had not studied hard, I'd never have become a doctor. But I believed that God had spoken to me about being a doctor, so I worked hard to see that happen. And yes, it tired me out! If I'd failed, would that have made me a failure? No. But it may have called into question whether I had heard God correctly about what he wanted me to do with my life.

Sometimes, to achieve something is hard work and we just have to knuckle down and do it. God never said this life would be easy. But we do need to weigh the resolutions we make in the light of what God wants. Sometimes, we may be measuring against the wrong criteria for success and so we might need to adjust what is important. At the start of Ecclesiastes it says:

> *I have seen all the things that are done under the sun; all of them are meaningless, a chasing after the wind.*

> *Ecclesiastes 1:14 (NIVUK)*

Solomon had done all things, and was wise and rich, and yet he realised that he could strive much for all these things but they were as pointless as chasing after the wind.

Jesus puts it another way:

> *"Yes, I am the vine; you are the branches. Those who remain in me, and I in them, will produce much fruit. For apart from me you can do nothing."*

> *John 15:5 (NLT)*

There are some things that are more important, and keeping close to Jesus is the key one. When we are in the will of God, we will be able to do much; apart from him, it all becomes a chasing after the wind.

So where is your motivation? I started the chapter with the question, do I need to strive more? The answer is maybe, maybe not! The motivation behind what you are thinking about is so much more of an issue.

What is it you think you need to work harder at?

_____

_____

Why do you want to do that?

_____

_____

_____

What will change if you do it?

_____

_____

What does God say about that?

_____

_____

A bit like the feedback, we sometimes need to focus on the positives for a moment.

Ask friends what you are good at. What do they think is positive about you?

When you write references for someone, you have to be honest, but at the same time you don't mention the negatives. Write yourself a reference. Remember to include all the positive attributes that makes you suitable.

This is a reference for _____

_____

_____

_____

_____

_____

_____

_____

_____

_____

We don't always believe the positive things, and need to concentrate on them more. I find understanding who I am in God is very important in giving me a more level understanding about what I should be concentrating on. There is a Hillsong song that has the line, "I'm a child of God, yes I am." I find singing songs like that gain me so much perspective on where I should focus, because I am building on solid foundations.

Of course, the opposite can be true; you can strive to have much less than you currently are enjoying. This might be a good thing, if that is what God is telling you to go for (and I'd check with some wise friends first). But it could be negative depending again on your motivation. God might be encouraging you to go for a lot more than you are currently settling for, and so you might need to strive for that thing, working hard to see if it happens. God gifts us according to what he wants us to do for him.

In his fantastic book *Jesus + Nothing = Everything*, Tullian Tchividjian says:

> *Now you can spend your life giving up your place for others instead of guarding it from others, because your identity is in Christ, not in your place. Now you can spend your energy going to the back instead of getting to the front, because your identity is in Christ not in your position. You can also spend your life giving, not taking, because your identity is in Christ, not in your possessions. All this is your new identity*

– all because of Christ's finished work declared to us in the gospel.[1]

We need to find a balance between striving for more and seeking less, depending on what God is saying to us at any particular point in our life.

---

[1] *Jesus + Nothing = Everything;* p133

4

Why Don't I Stick to My Plans?

As I started to write this book there was a great flurry of activity; I am sure God challenged me to write despite the fact I have never done that before. I then preached on the topic to the church I go to.

Then I got rejected from the first publisher, mainly on the basis of the title. And I stopped. Nine months passed and little happened. God then had to nudge me again to get on with it.

When we are to do something, we can easily prevaricate; that is, to do something else that seems more appealing at the time and put off what we are supposed to be doing. It is also easy to be diverted by other things that seem interesting, or at least more interesting, than the task that we have been set, or set ourselves.

We often find that there is a lure of other 'priorities' instead of the thing we are supposed to be doing.

Why is it that these things happen?

I think there are a number of traps that we fall into.

Trap 1: We do it all in our own strength

When you have a plan, you obviously want to do that thing. It is so easy to then do it all according to your own ability. We are told in the Bible to...

> *Trust in the LORD with all your heart; do not depend on your own understanding. Seek his will in all you do, and he will show you which path to take.*
>
> *Proverbs 3:5-6 (NLT)*

But the thing is that we just forget about God and plough on. It's then that we start to rely in our own strength.

> *Commit everything you do to the LORD. Trust him, and he will help you.*
>
> *Psalm 37:5 (NLT)*

So first of all we need to stop, and ask for God's help.

What are you trying right now that's not working?

_____

_____

Do you need to commit that to God?

_____

Trap 2: When we try to do something that is in the will of God, the Devil is not happy, and wants to oppose us.

He will sit on your shoulder and whisper to you that you are not good enough, and that you will never succeed.

What lies do you think the Devil is whispering to you?

_____

_____

_____

In your own strength you may not succeed. And in your own strength you are not good enough to do anything. But you are not on your own. You were bought at a price.

Trap 3: When we think that we are not good enough, we will quickly start to worry and doubt.

This can easily become stronger, if we allow it, than what God actually says about us. You will begin to overcome your stronghold of worrying when you decide that what God says about you is more important than what you are believing.

What is worrying you?

_____

_____

_____

Jesus said:

> "I have told you all this so that you may have peace
> in me. Here on earth you will have many trials and
> sorrows. But take heart, because I have overcome
> the world."
>
> *John 16:33 (NLT)*

What did he tell the disciples? That he was in the Father, and the Father was in him. He also said he would send the Holy Spirit to comfort and guide us.

You are not alone!

Trap 4: Our plans or God's plans?

If we are operating from our own plans rather than what God has actually said, then we might not find it all goes smoothly. Look at Jonah; it didn't quite all go his way.

How do you know that what you are doing is what God has asked you to do?

_____

_____

_____

If it is not clear to you, then you need to pray and also ask someone wise to pray with you. See what God says to them.

Reading the Bible is also helpful here. If what you are planning does not line up with what the Bible says, then it won't be from God.

When we are trapped we need to find a ladder to help us out of the hole.

Ladder 1

What are the obstacles and barriers that are seemingly in the way of you doing what you think is right?

_____

_____

_____

It might be that the barriers are not barriers at all. It may be that there are things that need to be done in order for you to get the prize you are looking for.

Repeatedly in the Bible we read stories of people that seem to have hit a brick wall, or in Moses' case the Red Sea. Moses didn't start to teach everybody to swim at this point. Or try to make lots of floatation devices. He needed a bigger solution. God was in the provision of the miracle to remove the sea and make a dry path across for the million or so Israelites escaping the Egyptians.

Sometimes God wants us to embrace the challenge. Jesus did not succumb to eating the bread in the desert when the Devil was tempting him. God gave him the strength to overcome and win the battle.

Ladder 2

The writer to the Hebrews in the Bible encourages the reader to train their body like an athlete and throw off anything that would hinder them.[2] So they might need to take off the rucksack they are wearing, or the big walking boots, so they can put on trainers and run.

What do you need to get rid of?

_____

_____

This is quite a hard thing to do if we cannot see the prize of the goal. If we see the end goal then we are less likely to worry about having to work a bit to see what we can do to be fitter for the race.

I heard this illustration from Adrian Holloway at Newday in 2015:

> Imagine you could place a bet in 33AD on the story of twelve disciples perpetuating [the Church] or that the Roman Empire would wipe it out in a generation. You'd bet on the Romans. However, we name our children after those fishermen, and we name our dogs Nero and Caesar!

If the disciples had not been looking at the end goal and rather looked at the might of the Romans, they would have run away and hidden. But they had heard Jesus tell them to go to

---

[2] See Hebrews 12

all nations and tell everyone about him. That's what they focussed on instead.

Ladder 3

You were bought at a price. Jesus died to set you free. That makes you of infinite value. Yes you, a child of God, adopted into his family. When we realise who we are in God, then we can be free from what we think about ourselves.

John Piper says this about understanding the love of God for us. Bear with it as it a little complicated, but worth reading a couple of times.

> *The love of God is not God making much of us, but God's saving us from self-centeredness so that we can enjoy making much of Him forever. And our love to others is not our making much of them, but helping them to find satisfaction in making much of God. True love aims as satisfying people in the glory of God. Any love that terminates on man is eventually destructive. It does not lead people to the only lasting joy, namely, God. Love must be God-centred, or it is not true love; it leaves people without their final hope of joy.*

What is the thing that is of most value to you?

_____

_____

You are more valuable than that!

Ladder 4

The weather is never right! It is always too hot or too cold, too wet or too dry. We find ourselves often focussing on the negative thing. Why do we always discuss the negatives, when we focus on what's wrong and so can miss the point of what is good?

What is going wrong right now?

_____

_____

_____

_____

What is going right with these situations?

_____

_____

_____

_____

We need to focus on the good that God has intended for us, rather than be a pessimist. A fellow elder at my church, Phil, said, "What man and woman lost in the garden is intended to be restored to them. Namely, God's plan for their good." That is God's will.

> "For I know the plans I have for you," says the LORD. "They are plans for good and not for disaster, to give you a future and a hope."
>
> Jeremiah 29:11 (NLT)

That's what we need to remember when the sky looks grey.

But sometimes it is just a bit grey, and we need to be real that it is not always sunny in life. Pete Greig, in his fantastic book *God on Mute*, says:

> Perhaps your experiences of unanswered prayer have left you hurting and disorientated like Mary Magdalene. If so, he asks you the question he asked her, 'why are you crying?' so tell him. Lament. Rant, if you need to. And when you are done, stop and hear the way he speaks your name.[3]

This is not just Pete's advice, but is what we see David doing in the psalms. It's OK to rant at God about these things. But we must not stay disappointed. At the end of a psalm where it all seems to have gone wrong, David often turns around and finishes, "But you God are great, and I will praise you no matter what."

Maybe writing a psalm, your very own rant to God, would help get it out there and stop making you feel like it's a grey day.

---

[3] *God on Mute*, p297

Ladder 5

The last of the ladders are idols. It's very easy for something else to take the place of God. In his book *Jesus + Nothing = Everything*, Tullian Tchividjian asks:

> So what are you trusting in, other than Jesus, to gain acceptance, or approval, to experience security and significance, to find meaning and purpose, to discover identity and direction?[4]

What are you trusting in rather than trusting in God?

_____

_____

When we realise what might be idols to us, then we can start to get rid of them. Timothy Keller, in his book called *Idols*, says:

> We think that idols are bad things, but that is almost never the case. The greater the good, the more likely we are to expect that it can satisfy our deepest needs and hopes. Anything can serve as a counterfeit God, especially the very best things in life. What is an idol? It is anything that is more important to you than God, anything that absorbs your heart and imagination more than God, anything you seek to give you what only God can give. A counterfeit God is anything so central and

---

[4] *Jesus + Nothing = Everything;* p41

essential to your life that, should you lose it, your life would hardly be worth living. An idol has such a controlling position in your heart that you can spend most of your passion and energy, your emotional and financial resources, on it without a second thought. If anything becomes more fundamental than God to your happiness, meaning in life, and identity, then it is an idol.

What is the thing you think about the most?

_____

_____

Jesus said:

"Where your treasure is, there your heart will be also."

Matthew 6:21 (NIV)

If we are thinking mainly about other things, we need to refocus on Jesus, and we will be surprised how easy it seems to not be in the hole anymore.

5

Why Do I Do the Things I Don't Want to Do?

If you struggle with sin, then the voice in your head will have said to you, "There you are. You are so crap because if you were a proper Christian you would not have done that."

You feel condemned and worthless as a result.

The problem is that this is all about your performance. We will never be able to perform well enough to gain respect from God. If we could, we would all be following the Law.

The apostle Paul says in Romans:

> I do not understand what I do. For what I want to do I do not do, but what I hate I do. For I do not do the good I want to do, but the evil I do not want to do – this I keep on doing. Now if I do what I do not want to do, it is no longer I who do it, but it is sin living in me that does it.

> Romans 7:15,19-20 (NIVUK)

Now that's a lots of dos and don'ts and takes a few re-readings to get your head around. The key to this is that Paul struggled too! You are not alone. And Paul was the guy who wrote half the New Testament and planted loads of churches. You are in good company if you struggle with sin. But his conclusion is that it is the sin that causes the problem.

Traditional church talks about the seven deadly sins. And my suspicion is that whatever you do, that the devil accuses you of, falls into one of these.

So what are they?

1. Lust

This is a real 'biggie' in the twenty-first century. Wherever you are in the world there are members of the opposite sex. There are also available all kinds of ways of seeing them naked. Pornography is more accessible than it has ever been.

There are scary statistics on how much it is viewed. A study by *provenmen.org* showed that two thirds of men in the US admit to viewing pornography at least every month, and Christian men nearly as often. In the same study 30% of men in the eighteen to thirty age group view pornography on a daily basis. Among Christians this is 7%. Amongst women the daily viewing figures are slightly lower at 3% and 1% of Christian women.

> *Run from anything that stimulates youthful lusts.*
> *Instead, pursue righteous living, faithfulness, love,*
> *and peace.*
>
> *2 Timothy 2:22 (NLT)*

The big question is, why do you look? What will it achieve? A quick, cheap thrill? But what will the longer lasting effect be? We all know the damage it does to relationships and to the ability to see the opposite sex as having value.

The thing is, there will always be the temptation to look. Our children are taught that if you stumble across something on the Internet by accident, you turn off the screen or close the page as soon as possible. I remember PJ Smythe saying once, "Bounce your eyes." If someone walks past with a low-cut top, or a very short skirt on, don't linger in your looking. This will help you not to lust. The lingering starts to make you lust, and that can lead to all kinds of problems.

So what can you do about lust or pornography?

The Bible talks about confessing your sins to one another. Whom can you trust with keeping you accountable? It needs to be someone who won't tell others but will ask you difficult questions and persist. It's not that they then judge you, but rather that they keep you on the right side of the line.

You could let someone have a regular report from your router that says what you have visited. Or let them have access to your Internet history another way.

Some service providers, phone and Internet, will let you limit what you can see. If the router they provide will not allow that, do you need to be as radical as changing provider, or even turning it off altogether?

Jesus is as radical as telling you to pluck out your eye if it causes you to sin. He meant that metaphorically, so hands off that knife! But some of the above measures may feel as bad to you and yet keep your sight healthy.

2. Gluttony

Overindulging is normal in our society. We don't drink; we get drunk. We don't eat because we need to, but because we want to and we can.

Obesity is not only a massive issue in the Western world, but is growing across Asia and Africa.

You might say, "But I can't help myself..."

How do you feel about the concept of fasting? That might just tell you something about your attitude to food.

> *Therefore, whether you eat or drink, or whatever you do, do all to the glory of God.*
>
> *1 Corinthians 10:31 (NKJV)*

So how do you eat a nice meal to the glory of God? Giving God glory is about it honouring God. If you eat till you can eat no more, and waddle from the table, does that honour God? If you enjoy the food and praise God for the mastery of both the chef and the natural bounty he has provided that chef, it may be a different story.

So the big question is, why do you do it? Is not God everything you need?

We all need to eat, but we don't need to do it to excess.

I remember a particularly large lady in hospital, who was so big she could not have investigations as the operating table could not take her weight. Even in hospital she was not losing weight, and she'd been spied drinking Mars Bar drinks between meals smuggled in by her relatives. One day when she said, "I cannot lose weight," the professor could not hold it in anymore and said to her, "There were no fat people in Belsen." The shock of all the team standing round her hospital bed was palpable, and as he walked away, she started to cry. The turning point for her started that day, as the enormity of her addiction to food hit her.

It may be that you need the discipline of recording everything. There was an interesting study that showed that when we do that, we underestimate the amount we are eating by a third. So you might even need to go to the length of recording the weight of what you eat as well as the calories it contains. There are great apps to help do this, so it's a lot easier than it used to be. Support is fantastic, and weight loss groups can help as they (like with lust) give accountability.

It may be that you feel that this issue is for you an addiction. If so, we need to ask the questions that Tullian Tchividjian asks:

> *Fundamentally somebody's worst addiction is no different from whatever issues of restlessness you and I face. And the first question I always ask is always the same: What are we really after? Inside us, what truly needs to be there that isn't? It might be acceptance or approval, in various ways, from various people. It could be a sense of direction or significance or purpose. It may well be the experience of security or of freedom and deliverance. We're looking for these things all the time.*[5]

3. Greed

This is similar to lust and gluttony as it is all about having enough. However, there are some facts in life:

- You will never have enough.

---

[5] *Jesus + Nothing = Everything;* p36

- You will always earn too little. Most people spend about 10% more than they earn.
- Other people will always have more than you. Even Bill Gates is not top of the world rich list, and others have more than the Sultan of Brunei.

Let your conduct be without covetousness; be content with such things as you have. For He Himself has said, 'I will never leave you nor forsake you.'

Hebrews 13:5 (NKJV)

So this says, don't lust after more things but be content. And this comes with a promise: that God will always be with you.

Spending plans and budgets might help, and once again, accountability with what you are spending or desiring to spend may help here.

What you have will never be the best, until you change your thinking.

God has the best for you. Do you really believe that? Jesus says he does not give you a scorpion when you ask for an egg. However, he doesn't give you cake either! So at this point you might think, "Well, I'll ask for cake then!" But God gives according to your need, not your wants.

4. Sloth (Laziness)

God did not make us to do little, but to be productive. There seem to be two extremes in modern life. The most common is not resting. That was the idea of the Sabbath: a day of rest. If you are not resting, you need to diarise some time to stop. We all need rest and we all have limits. If you are pushing too hard, one day the engine will blow. That includes doing church work...

However, sometimes the issue is the laziness. If this is an issue you may need to make a plan as to what to do – and stick to it!

> *Take a lesson from the ants, you lazybones. Learn from their ways and become wise!*
>
> *Proverbs 6:6 (NLT)*

Ants rarely rest, but continue to work for the good of the community. They take no time to watch TV or play computer games.

Once again, accountability may help you if you struggle with this.

5. Wrath (Anger)

It's very easy to get wound up by people and for anger to spill out.

> *Never pay back evil with more evil. Do things in such a way that everyone can see you are honorable. Do all that you can to live in peace with everyone. Dear friends, never take revenge. Leave that to the righteous anger of God. For the Scriptures say,*
>   *"I will take revenge;*
>   *I will pay them back,"*
>   *says the LORD.*
>
> *Romans 12:17-19 (NLT)*

We need to trust God to deal with people in a just and fair way, and not get angry. Easier said than done.

There are many other outlets for the anger. My favourite two are exercise and prayer. They often come at the same time! My fastest bike routes are often after a bad day at work. God often speaks to me as I tell him how unjust certain things are, and it's a lot easier to let go when I have heard his voice.

6. Envy

Envy is wanting what other people have. That may be things, or positions they hold, or respect they have. The root of this is that you don't trust in God to provide for your needs. What they have is always better. Their donkey, wife, food.

Even in the desert God provided for his people. He will provide for you. Believing that can be quite tricky. But we need to start to try. Again, telling him might be a start.

> *A sound heart is life to the body,*
> *But envy is rottenness to the bones.*
>
> Proverbs 14:30 (NKJV)

It will eat you if you allow it to.

7. Pride

This is the final of the 'seven deadly sins'. Pride is self-belief. If we believe in ourselves, then we are not trusting in God. That is a dangerous place to be. We need to trust in God in such a way that we boast in what God has done, is doing, or will do.

In his song called *Gracious*, Simon Brading talks about these very kind of issues, and how great God is at dealing with them. I love it and it is the kind of song I listen to if I struggle with something.

Time and time again
I'm feeling like I've failed You
I've let down a friend, my heart aches
Tried it on my own
Ended up in pieces
Nothing good to show, I need You

What if Your love is bigger than my mess?
What if Your grace can heal my brokenness?
In all the world and universe
You specialise in failures
And oh, You are gracious
And You take my mess, nail it to a cross
Broken lives will rise again
Broken years restored again
And oh, You are gracious
And You make my life a trophy of grace
There is healing in Your wounds
Forgiveness for the sinner
Mercy leads me to repentance
I turn my face to find a Father who is gracious
No anger in Your eyes
But mercy
Gracious is the name of the Lord
Gracious is the name of the Lord our God

I know Your love is bigger than my mess
I know Your grace can heal my brokenness

Simon Brading; copyright © 2014

The Bible says that sin entangles so easily. Although that is true, God's grace undoes the sin too. That involves no effort on our part. When we realise what Jesus has done for us, we also want to flee from sin.

In Romans 6, Paul talks about sin and our struggles with it. He focuses in on sexual sin especially, as that one was so much of a problem in the first century church, just as it is today.

He starts off by saying, "Well, if there is grace for us when we sin, should we therefore not worry and just go on sinning?"

> *What shall we say then? Are we to continue in sin that grace may abound?*
>
> *Romans 6:1 (ESV)*

His response is clear.

> *By no means! How can we who died to sin still live in it? Do you not know that all of us who have been baptized into Christ Jesus were baptized into his death? We were buried therefore with him by baptism into death, in order that, just as Christ was raised from the dead by the glory of the Father, we too might walk in newness of life.*
>
> *Romans 6:2-4 (ESV)*

So we should not sin, as we are new creations. Now we know, as I have said above, that by the next chapter he is saying, "I know I struggle with sin too." So he is not saying as a Christian we will never sin. What he is saying is that in Christ, by the power of the Holy Spirit, we have the power not to sin.

He says:

> *Let not sin therefore reign in your mortal body, to make you obey its passions. Do not present your members to sin as instruments for unrighteousness, but present yourselves to God as those who have been brought from death to life, and your members to God as instruments for righteousness. For sin will have no dominion over you, since you are not under law but under grace. What then? Are we to sin because we are not under law but under grace? By no means! Do you not know that if you present yourselves to anyone as obedient slaves, you are slaves of the one whom you obey, either of sin, which leads to death, or of obedience, which leads to righteousness?*
>
> *Romans 6:12-16 (ESV)*

It's an odd concept, being a slave to doing good things (righteousness) rather than sin. Most of us would struggle with the concept that we are slaves to sin, although we might possibly recognise it when we struggle with sin, because it controls us. But Jesus has won the war on sin, and we can do it too in his strength. So his advice as to how to avoid it is, just don't go there!

When Paul writes to the Corinthian people, he has to address the fact that they are going off to see prostitutes. There were some people in the church arguing that they could because they were made clean by the work of Christ on the cross.

> *'I have the right to do anything,' you say – but not everything is beneficial. 'I have the right to do anything' – but I will not be mastered by anything.*
>
> *1 Corinthians 6:12 (NIVUK)*

He says, "No, stop, just don't go there!" Then he goes on in verse 18 to say, "Run away! Flee from sin!" Sometimes we need to flee to be free.

All of this would be a lot easier if we understood our identities.

When John writes his Gospel, right at the start he establishes that if you know Jesus then you are a child of God.

> *But to all who did receive him, who believed in his name, he gave the right to become children of God...*
>
> *John 1:12 (ESV)*

You are a child of God. That makes you royalty. Yes, *you!* You are a prince or a princess.

If you were prime minister tomorrow, you'd know that everything you tweeted, posted, said and looked at would be known. It would change your behaviour.

Being a child of God should be similar.

You have been made righteous.

It doesn't matter which sin you struggle with, the truth is that all of the sins are based in the lie that God will not provide for all of your needs. If you trust God wholeheartedly, that he will provide for all of your needs, then it will be a lot easier to stay further from sin. When you understand that you are a child of God, and so have all the resources and strength that being royal gives to you, you should find that it is easier to trust and obey.

There is a spiritual battle for your identity! The Devil does not want you to know who you are, because that will make you a stronger Christian, and so much more of a threat to his ways.

So how can you be free?

1. Tell someone.
2. Start everyday with the vow, "I won't." Maybe have a reminder on your mirror or by your toothbrush, and agree with God in the morning that you will not.
3. Maybe change something that makes it more likely that you will slip.
4. When you slip, remember that God loves you and has forgiven you. Jesus has already died for your sins.
5. Remember, you will be free of this in heaven.

After the bit in Ephesians 6 about putting on the armour of God, it says:

> *Finally, be strong in the Lord and in the strength of his might.*

> *Ephesians 6:10 (ESV)*

We can put the armour on and it will protect us. But remember, it is *his* armour and *his* strength, not ours.

We need to remember that Jesus was tempted. Temptation is not wrong. It's what we do with it.

If you are struggling with temptations and sins, make a list of them on the opposite page.

Temptations/sins:

_____

_____

_____

_____

_____

_____

What does the Devil say about you and your sin?

_____

_____

What does he whisper in your ear?

_____

_____

Then in response to that, what does God say about you?

_____

_____

I can assure you, the things God says about you will overcome anything the Devil can say. You will find freedom in the promises of God. If you cannot find truths to counteract what the Devil has said, find an older Christian to help you.

Mark Driscoll explains it like this:

> For the Christian, there is a vital difference between having sin and being sin. This explains why the bible rarely, if ever, describes a Christian, as opposed to a non-Christian, as a sinner. Depending upon which bible translation you read, you will hear of non-Christians referred to as sinners more than 300 times, but only on 3 occasions do you find a Christian referred to as a sinner, though in each instance it may refer to a non-Christian. Rather than sinners, the bible overwhelmingly calls us saints, holy or righteous more than 200 times. Basically, then, the primary identity of a believer in Christ is not a sinner but a saint. While we still struggle with sin in this life, as Christians, our identity is not found in our sin but in Christ's righteousness.[6]

Isn't that exciting? We are free from sin despite the fact we may feel like we struggle with it. Jesus has won the battle already.

> The temptations in your life are no different from what others experience. And God is faithful. He will not allow the temptation to be more than you can

---

[6] *Who Do You Think You Are?* p35

stand. When you are tempted, he will show you a way out so that you can endure.

1 Corinthians 10:13 (NLT)

6

Am I Actually Hopeless?

We have considered a lot of questions together. At this point some of you might still be thinking, "But the problem is, I really am never going to be anything but bottom of the pile."

Are you at the bottom of your class in every subject? Well, maybe you do have a problem with learning, and if so you need to find that out so you can get professional help.

If you aren't the bottom of every class, what aren't you so bad at? Could you apply yourself more in that?

If you do have a disability that means you struggle in one area, what is it that you are good at? You might have no legs that work, but that doesn't mean that you aren't funny, or loving, or clever. Maybe you'll never read and write, but that does not mean you can't be a really good carpenter.

Think of a skill or something you do.

If you put yourself in a line, with all the people of the world, all eight billion of them, where would you rank in the skill you are thinking of? Mark yourself on the line.

_____

Bottom   Top

I would guess you are maybe in the middle somewhere.

If you are really quite good, you might make it into the top billion. That's equivalent to being one of the best three in an average class.

Top million, you say? That means in a group of eight thousand people, you'd be the top. So in a small town, you'd be the best at what you are thinking of. Most of us would not be there!

The opposite is also true. The lowest million. You'd be the worst in your town. Most of us can think of others who would be worse at something. It might be your granny, or a newborn baby, but you are definitely not down there!

So most of us are really quite average, and if we really excel, we are still in a huge group of people who are similar. Therefore, you might say that none of us are that special.

But in God's eyes, you are really special. He made you, and he loves you for who you are. When we really understand that, we will start to have some perspective on how we feel.

I love driving. If I were a Formula One driver and I was three seconds off the pace and at the back of the grid, would that make me a rubbish driver? No, it wouldn't. I'd still be one of the world's top drivers, otherwise I wouldn't be able to be on the grid in the first place. So why do those drivers keep going? They have the belief they can win. With the right car, and the right tyres and weather, they have the belief they could be the best.

A footballer in league 2 will believe they are good enough for the premiership, but maybe they have just not had the break. They are not rubbish just because they are three leagues from the top.

In the *Eddie the Eagle* film, when he is having a really bad day, his father says to him, "You will never be an Olympian."

That motivates him to work harder, and eventually he gets there, as the all-time worst ski jumper ever known at the Olympics.

If you practise most things you will improve. It does not mean everyone can be a great artist or sportsperson, but you may be quite good.

You might think, "That's well and good, but I'll never be able to participate in an elite sport." That may be true. I never will either. But the question should be, do you need to be good at something to get pleasure from it or give pleasure to others? I do believe that there is a lot more to life than being the best. If it were not so, none of us would compete in any sports at all.

When we do exams, the average grade is a C, not an A. For most of life, average is good enough.

A badly made bird box may bring you pleasure when you see the birds nesting in it, flying in and out feeding their chicks. A really rather average freezer meal being devoured by your children who say, "That was really good!" will bring you pleasure, even though it would never win a *MasterChef* cook off. You don't have to be the best to enjoy things in life. It's all a matter of perspective.

Genesis 1:27 says you were made in God's image. So you have his (i.e. God's) attributes!

Phil, one of the elders at my church, once said, "You are fearfully and wonderfully made, so stop wishing you were someone or somewhere else." He went on to say, "There are lots of people in the Bible who did amazing things but we don't even know their names."

Sometimes we might be struggling because we are depressed, and then we might not be able to see the positives that are there. I would suggest a couple of things. The first is, have you seen the doctor? They might suggest medications or counselling. Either way, God wants you to have a different perspective. There may be many reasons you are not feeling happy about life. But there are many positives that will help you think differently.

> *Don't copy the behaviour and customs of this world, but let God transform you into a new person by changing the way you think. Then you will learn to know God's will for you, which is good and pleasing and perfect.*
>
> *Romans 12:2 (NLT)*

So it is worth just thinking for a moment...

What gives me the greatest sense of worth?

_____

_____

What do I enjoy most?

_____

What is it that I do, that gives others pleasure?

_____

_____

A chap called Stef Liston said, "A wasp without a sting is a stripy fly." The fact is, the fly does not know it does not have a sting. The world keeps telling us that we are incomplete because we don't have a sting, but we were never made to have one. Maybe you just need to realise you are a fly, not a wasp.

> *Far from being an accident, you and I are part of a brilliant plan that started before planet Earth and continues beyond it. This is why self-deprecation is as wicked as slandering God's Church. We are belittling the creation of something God has planned and crafted. He chose us before the foundation of the world, knew us before He made us (Jer. 1:5), and drew up works for us before we were even created (Eph. 2:10). He had plans for His sacred Church and included us in those plans. This thought should bring tremendous peace to our often-stressed souls. The more I think about it, the more honoured I feel to be chosen as part of God's eternal plan for the Church.[7]*

This was put so well I had to include it. We have to change our perspective on who we are and why we are here if we are to have purpose.

My friend Marion said to me on a day I was feeling particularly unhappy, "Keep your head up, or your crown will drop off." We forget that we are princes and princesses in the Kingdom of God so quickly. We let our head droop, and before we know it, our crowns are slipping.

---

[7] Francis Chan; *Letters to the Church;* #3

I was skiing with a good friend Martin. Our instructor said to him, "Martin, look up, look at the view." Martin was concentrating so much on what he was doing with his skis, he had forgotten where he was in the beautiful mountains.

Look up!

7

Maybe I'm Not So Crap After All?

We have considered lots of questions together. I hope that this has helped you to work out what your point on this earth is.

You might have discovered that your whole point on this earth is to be an Olympic athlete... though the likelihood is that you have actually discovered that it is *not* to be. Whatever it is that you do, the likelihood is that the average grime artist, TV presenter or football ace is unlikely to be able to do what you do.

You are uniquely placed to be you. You are special, and perfect for where you are. That's why you have been made that way. What we need to be is the best that we can be for the role that we have been given. That might be being the best friend to the girl in the class that everyone calls smelly. It might be emptying people's bins with a smile or cleaning that toilet so well that people will never feel it is dirty. It might be designing the next website so well that the business you are working for increases its market share. Whatever it is, we need to be the best we can with what we have been given and accept our shortfalls.

Imagine if no-one did your job. What would be the consequence of that? What would be the effect on others?

A lot of how we feel is all about the way we picture ourselves, and the reality is that we don't necessarily see ourselves as others do.

In the 1950's a Methodist preacher called Norman Vincent-Peale wrote a book called *The Power of Positive Thinking*. At the time, the book was seen as outrageous as it was all about thinking differently. We had to get into the late part of the twentieth century before people caught up with his theology and ideas. Norman was ahead of his time in his explanation of where the Bible and psychology met. Imagine if he had let this put him off and he had never published!

What are you putting off because you are worried whether it will work, or be accepted?

_____

_____

We need to grapple with the tension of 'how can I be the best me' at the same time as 'how to live with myself as I am'.

What is God's name for you?

_____

God calls you his child. There is no truth more secure than you are a child of the King!

I read this on *compassion.com*, and it puts this better than I can:

God doesn't divvy out His love to us in small portions. Instead He pours out His love into our hearts. Very rarely will someone die for someone they merely respect, but occasionally someone will die for someone they love. That's what makes God's love for us so evident! Jesus died for us while we were still sinners, hating God and in rebellion of Him. His love extended to those who are most unworthy of it. He willingly took the punishment for our sins. He gave the most He could give to those who deserved it the least.

You may feel like nobody, but to God you are somebody. He chose to send His Son to die for you! What a great demonstration of our value and worth. In fact, God's Word says that when we place our trust in Him as our Saviour, He makes us God's children and co-heirs with Him. No matter what comes into our lives, He is there and His love is always available to us.

Our identity changes when we become God's children. True freedom and self-worth are found only in Christ. Once you accept the truth of God's ultimate love, His opinion becomes more important than others'. Ultimately, it's the only opinion that matters.

Verse 10 from Colossians 2 is really helpful for us to be able to get some perspective on who we are and our purpose. It says:

So you also are complete through your union with Christ, who is the head over every ruler and authority.

Colossians 2:10 (NLT)

The NIVUK says:

...and in Christ you have been brought to fullness. He is the head over every power and authority.

Colossians 2:10 (NIVUK)

And in the ESV it says:

...and you have been filled in him, who is the head of all rule and authority.

Colossians 2:10 (ESV)

What we can see by these different versions is that the thing that Christ does for us before God is that he makes us complete; we are filled and have a fullness that makes us sufficient for our purpose. He gives us the authority that we don't naturally have to be whole and perfect for the job at hand.

I love cooking. Do my children always like my food? No. But sometimes their eyes light up and say, that's really good. That makes all the average meals worthwhile.

Do they laugh at every dad joke? No. They mainly groan. But do they sometimes cry with laughter? Oh yes. So, I continue. More often I laugh lots too, and that is a proper feel-good moment.

If I gave up at all the negatives then I would not get the benefit of the positive moments.

> *Don't copy the behaviour and customs of this world,*
> *but let God transform you into a new person by*
> *changing the way you think. Then you will learn to*
> *know God's will for you, which is good and pleasing*
> *and perfect.*
>
> *Romans 12:2 (NLT)*

As we start to rethink who we are, and what God has made us to be, and what he says about us, it starts to change our very being, our actions and the things we see around us.

So What?

You might wonder why I was so bold in the title of the book. Doesn't seem very Christian! But this was the question I asked God. I don't usually swear. But God was not offended; he answered me.

And the apostle Paul used the same word when he wrote to the Philippians. You see, Paul gained some perspective as to what had value in his life.

> *What is more, I consider everything a loss because of the surpassing worth of knowing Christ Jesus my Lord, for whose sake I have lost all things. I consider them garbage, that I may gain Christ.*
>
> *Philippians 3:8 (NIVUK)*

The word 'garbage' was actually 'crap', 'poo', 'excrement'. He knew what was important. Nothing else was as important in his life as knowing Christ.

Tullian Tchividjian said in his book *Jesus + Nothing = Everything*:

> *Because Jesus was strong for me, I was free to be weak*
> *Because Jesus won for me, I was free to lose.*
> *Because Jesus was someone, I was free to be no one.*
> *Because Jesus was extraordinary, I was free to be ordinary.*

Because Jesus succeeded for me, I was free to fail.[8]

When we change our perspective, we can start to see what is important.

When we realise where our identity lies, we will be a lot more effective in our walk with God.

So I finish with a prayer Paul wrote to the Philippians. My wife and I have this inscribed on the inside of our wedding rings, and it is my prayer for so many people I come into contact with through the fantastic thing that is church.

> *And this is my prayer: that your love may abound more and more in knowledge and depth of insight, so that you may be able to discern what is best and may be pure and blameless for the day of Christ, filled with the fruit of righteousness that comes through Jesus Christ – to the glory and praise of God.*
>
> Philippians 1:9-11 (NIVUK)

---

[8] *Jesus + Nothing = Everything*; p24

Resources

In the book I have quoted from a few different books. If you want to look a bit further into these topics, then here is a summary to help you find the right place to get more information.

Jesus + Nothing = Everything. Tullian Tchividian. Published by Crossway.

This is a great book looking at why we always want to do things for Jesus, but that we are not required to. How do we get out of that trap?

God on Mute. Pete Greig. Published by David C. Cook.

This is the best book on unanswered prayer I have ever read. Peter started the 24/7 prayer movement and has written a number of books on the topic.

Who Do You Think You Are? Mark Driscoll. Published by Thomas Nelson.

This is a slightly harder read, but takes the reader through all the things they are in Christ, like a saint, blessed, appreciated etc. It is worth a look if you are still struggling to accept your identity in Christ.

Letters to the Church. Francis Chan.

This is a book, but also has a website, YouTube channel and a reading plan in the YouVersion Bible app. Francis is a great communicator. In this he looks at lots of the letters in the Bible, and speaks a lot about our identity and purpose.

If you prefer to listen, then *Look Up, Child* by Lauren Daigle is available to download or stream. It has some great songs on this album which point us back to Christ when we find we are bogged down by what the world says about us.

Contact the Author

To contact the author, please write to:

Peter Williams
c/o Onwards and Upwards Publishers Ltd.
4 The Old Smithy
London Road
Rockbeare
Exeter
EX5 2EA

Or send an email to:

WAISC@churchinthepeak.org

More information about the author can be found
on the book's web page:

www.onwardsandupwards.org/why-am-i-so-crap

Related Books from the Publisher

Well Done, Good and Faithful Servant
Steve Pollard
978-1-78815-720-9

The Christian life is a marathon, not a sprint. This valuable resource will help you to keep up the pace, avoid obstacles and stay focused on the prize. Learn how to become the person God has designed you to be – impacting your relationships, your actions and your sense of purpose.

What Happened After Mr Jones Died
Paul Wreyford
978-1-78815-731-5

Mr Jones didn't have a good Christmas. He died. Not to worry – he's a Christian, so he's going to heaven... isn't he? Mr Gilmore, his guardian angel, thinks so... but Demon Dumas doesn't. The matter is referred to a celestial court, where a jury of twelve dead men and women must decide whether there is enough evidence to prove that Mr Jones is a Christian. What follows is the most astonishing case in the history of the afterlife.

Books available from all good bookshop
and from **www.onwardsandupwards.org**